# THIS BOOK BELONGS TO:

_____

_____

_____

# Before you unleash your creativity...

*Thank you for choosing my coloring book.*
*All the illustrations have been drawn by free hand*
*from a blank page, just for you!*

## YOUR FUN AT THE FIRST PLACE

Coloring is a great activity that can help to relax and have a good time with yourself. You can do it when you want and how you want it. There is not a wrong way, just your way!

## COLORING TIPS

The paper used by Amazon is perfect for soft colored pencils, gel pens or alcohol based markers. If you use wet tools, don't forget to place a blank sheet behind the page you're coloring to prevent any bleed-through that may occur. You can find a color test page at the beginning of the book where you can test your colors and get the perfect palette for each image.

## SHARE YOUR MASTERPIECE

You're very welcome to share your finished colored masterpieces on social media and on the coloring communities online. Please don't forget to include my name and the book title, it would be a great support for my work and future coloring books.

## Join Our Special Coloring United Community

Feel free to write to me for any feedback and collaboration at
*coloringunited@gmail.com*

# COLOR TEST PAGE

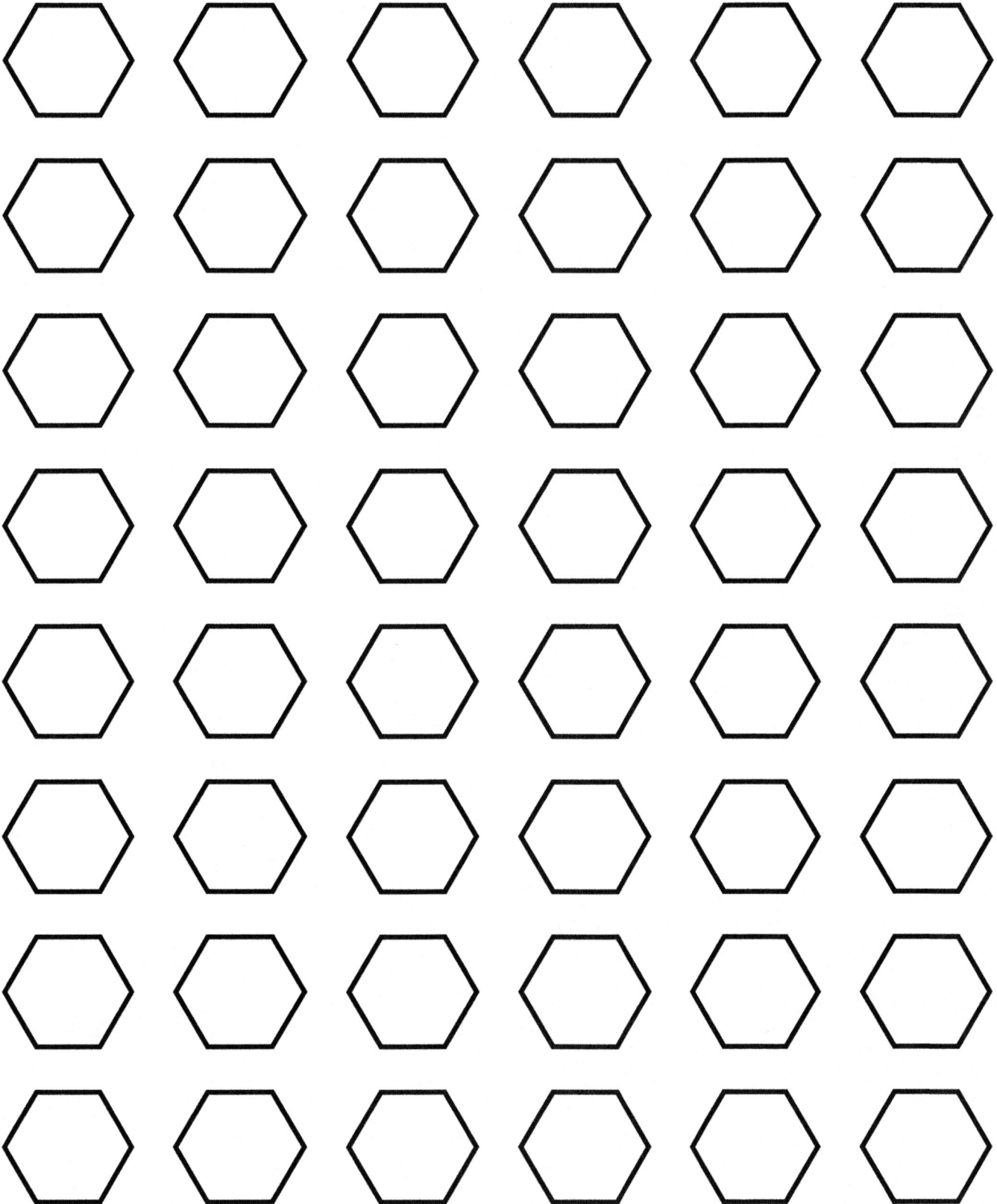

# DID YOU ENJOY COLORING THIS BOOK?

We appreciate your feedback!
Please write a review on Amazon,
it helps me and other coloring fans.

## PLEASE SHARE YOUR EXPERIENCE

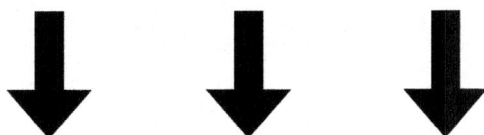

**Review this product**

Share your thoughts with other customers

Write a customer review

THANK YOU!

Printed in Great Britain
by Amazon